The future of our Yesterday

written by, Amor Strong
illustrated by, Anwargart

The Future Of Our Yesterday
Published By From Prison With Love Publishing Company LLC
Pub Name: Amor Strong

To my most favorite girls in the whole wide world,

**Daddy loves you, and I know this time we've spent
apart hasn't been easy,
but please believe me when I say it wasn't taken for
granted.
I pray from here on, our life is nothing but cupcakes
and rainbows.**

**With love,
Dad**

Alivia was a cute little six-year-old girl. She lived with her mom and older sister Aja. Aja was eleven years old, but despite the age gap, they were the best of friends. Some time ago, Alivia's dad had lived with them too. But now, her dad was in prison. She missed her dad a lot.

Aja had a different dad. Sometimes, she went to visit him on the weekends. This particular weekend, Aja was going camping. She just could not stop talking about it!
"It's going to be awesome!" she told Alivia. "Maybe you can come with me too, Livi. Dad always tells me to bring you along."

"I can't, Sissy…" Alivia said sadly. "I'm going to visit my daddy on Saturday."
"Oh," Aja said. "I know how much you have been wanting to see him. Still, I do wish you could go camping with us too." "We can all go camping together when Daddy comes home," Alivia said. "I hope it happens soon."

And so, Aja's dad came to pick her up on Saturday while Alivia and her mom went to the prison to see Alivia's dad. Just as usual, Alivia felt so sad to see her dad waiting for them in the visiting hall. He always looked forward to their visits. He would play board games and card games with Alivia when she came to visit.

"Hey, Mi Amor," Dad said with a bright smile. "I was waiting for you. How are you doing? How is school?" Alivia knew that 'Mi Amor' meant 'My Love'. "School is great!" said Alivia. "We went to the aquarium this week and I got to see the clownfish!" Dad listened to everything Alivia had to say. "I wish I could be with you. It makes me feel really bad. But I have to smile because I don't want you to feel bad too."

After Alivia told her dad everything about her week, it was Mom's turn. Alivia waited patiently until her mom and dad finished talking. Suddenly, a buzzer went off. Visiting times were over. "Well, I guess it's time for us to say goodbye," said Alivia's mom. "Never goodbye," Alivia's dad shook his head. "Goodbye is forever. This is more like a see you later."

"Daddy, do you have to go?" Alivia asked, a tear forming in her eyes. "It's not fair!" "We can see each other again," Dad reminded her. "I'm making a list of all the wonderful things we will do when I get out. Besides, I did something bad, and I'm being punished for it. This is a good lesson for me to never do bad things again."

"You'd better not!" said Alivia strictly. "I just miss you so much, Daddy. I want you to come back home soon." "Yes. Every time I go back to my cell, I can't stop thinking about you. I want to spend more time with you, and I feel so sad when I have to leave you. I promise I will be a good person when I get out, for your sake."
8

Tearfully, they bid goodbye to each other.
Alivia watched as her dad went away,
hoping to see him again soon.

9

On Monday, Aja came back from her camping trip. She had so many amazing things to tell Alivia and their mom. "We had lots and lots of fun!" Aja exclaimed. "We camped in the middle of the woods near a beautiful stream. At night, we could hear all the sounds of the woods! The bats were screeching, the bugs were chirping, the owls were hooting, and the leaves were rustling... We could see so many stars in the sky!"

"That sounds amazing…" Alivia said thoughtfully. She could almost imagine herself and her dad camping together. "Dad told me stories about the stars," said Aja. "Did you know that all the constellations have really cool stories?" Alivia shook her head.

"I will tell you all about them!" said Aja. "Oh, and we roasted marshmallows over a campfire and watched fireflies!" The more Alivia kept listening to Aja, the sadder she felt. She was upset that she could not do any of those activities with her dad.

"It's okay," she told herself. "We can go camping when Daddy comes back." That night, Alivia prayed to God, asking to see her dad back home soon. She wanted to spend time with her dad so much! While she was sleeping, she felt God's presence and knew that everything was going to be alright.

Alivia spent the next week thinking about all the amazing things she would do with her dad. Aja just could not stop talking about all the fun she had with her dad. "I also had lots of fun with Daddy before he went away," Alivia told Aja one day at breakfast. "He brought me a colorful mermaid cake for my birthday! Then he made me breakfast! We also went riding on a horsey. Oh, and a bird pooped on Dad's shoulder while he was hanging the pinata! It was so funny!"

"Wow!" said Aja, her eyes bright. Alivia saw her Mom looking at her in confusion. "Are you sure you went horseback riding with Daddy? Was there a mermaid birthday cake? Hmm, I'm trying to remember when your dad made breakfast for you on your birthday. I have to ask your Daddy; he'll surely remember.

That weekend, Alivia visited her dad once again. Just like usual, Dad was so happy to see Alivia. "It's so good to see you, Mi Amor," Dad told her with a smile. "How have you been?" "I've been good, Daddy!" Alivia beamed. "I have so many great memories to think about." "That's good then," Dad said. "Can you tell me about the memories that make you happy?"

"Sure!" Alivia said, sitting up straight. "Daddy, do you remember when you got me a colorful mermaid cake? Or when you made pancakes, bacon, and eggs for my breakfast. And then we rode on a horsey! Then a bird pooped on your shoulder while you hung the pinata!" "Well, people say that it brings good luck when a bird poops on you," her dad said with a smile.

"Really?" Alivia asked. "Do you remember that day, Daddy?" Alivia's dad thoughtful for a while. He could not remember anything Alivia talked about! But he did not want to hurt her feelings. "Of course, I remember, baby girl," Alivia's dad said with a smile. "We had so much fun that day, didn't we?"

"Yes, we did!" Alivia said. "I'm so happy that you remember that day, Daddy." While Alivia and her mom continued to talk, Alivia's dad felt sad. He felt bad about himself and the lost time between them. Was Alivia creating false memories to cover for the time I wasn't there for her? She was so little when he went to prison, after all… So, there was no way she could remember anything from back then. "Livi, why don't you go and select a game for us to play?" asked Alivia's mom.

"Okay, Mommy," said Alivia, walking away.
"It's completely your fault!" Alivia's mom told her dad. "She's making up stories and false memories because of you. You should have been there for her."
"I know…" Alivia's dad said guiltily. "I'm so sorry…"
When it was time to say goodbye, all of them got tearful once again. Just like usual, Dad promised to come back home soon before he left.

After returning to his cell, Alivia's dad cried. He kept crying as he recalled what Alivia had said. "Please God," he said, falling to his knees. "Please give me the strength to be the man I need to be for my baby girl." That night, while he was sleeping, Alivia's dad heard God's voice. "Do not worry," God seemed to be saying. "Maintain faith in me and everything will be alright."

Alivia's dad did just that. He behaved well and looked forward to Alivia's visits. After a couple of months, he was released because he behaved so well. Needless to say, Alivia was so happy when her daddy came home. She hugged him tight and refused to let him go! She even insisted on sleeping in his bed to make sure that it wasn't all a dream.

"It's not a dream," Alivia's dad said as he kissed her on the forehead. "I'm really here. And I will never leave your side ever again! I love you so much and I want to spend all my time with you." "Me too, Daddy!" Alivia said. "I want to create lots and lots of amazing memories with you."

That night, Alivia and her dad sat on the porch, looking at the stars up in the sky. Dad showed Alivia two constellations named the Big Dipper and the Little Dipper. He told her that if she ever got lost, the North Star would lead her back home. "I'm so glad that you're here with me, Daddy," Alivia said. "I don't want anything to change. I want all of us to be happy together." "We will," her dad told her. "I promise!" Alivia could feel in her heart that his words were true.

A few days later, it was Alivia's birthday. That morning, her dad decided to make breakfast for her. He made pancakes, bacon, and eggs. While he cooked, Alivia's dad felt as if he had done the same thing before. Alivia was so happy to see that her dad had made breakfast for her. She was even more surprised when her magnificent birthday cake arrived.

It was the most beautiful and colorful mermaid cake she had ever seen! And later, Dad took her horseback riding. It was the most fun she had in her whole life. In the afternoon, they threw a birthday party. Alivia's friends and relatives came to wish her a happy birthday. Dad brought in a huge pinata full of her favorite candy. While he was hanging the pinata, a bird flew by and pooped on his shoulder! Everyone except Aja, dad, and Mom burst out laughing.

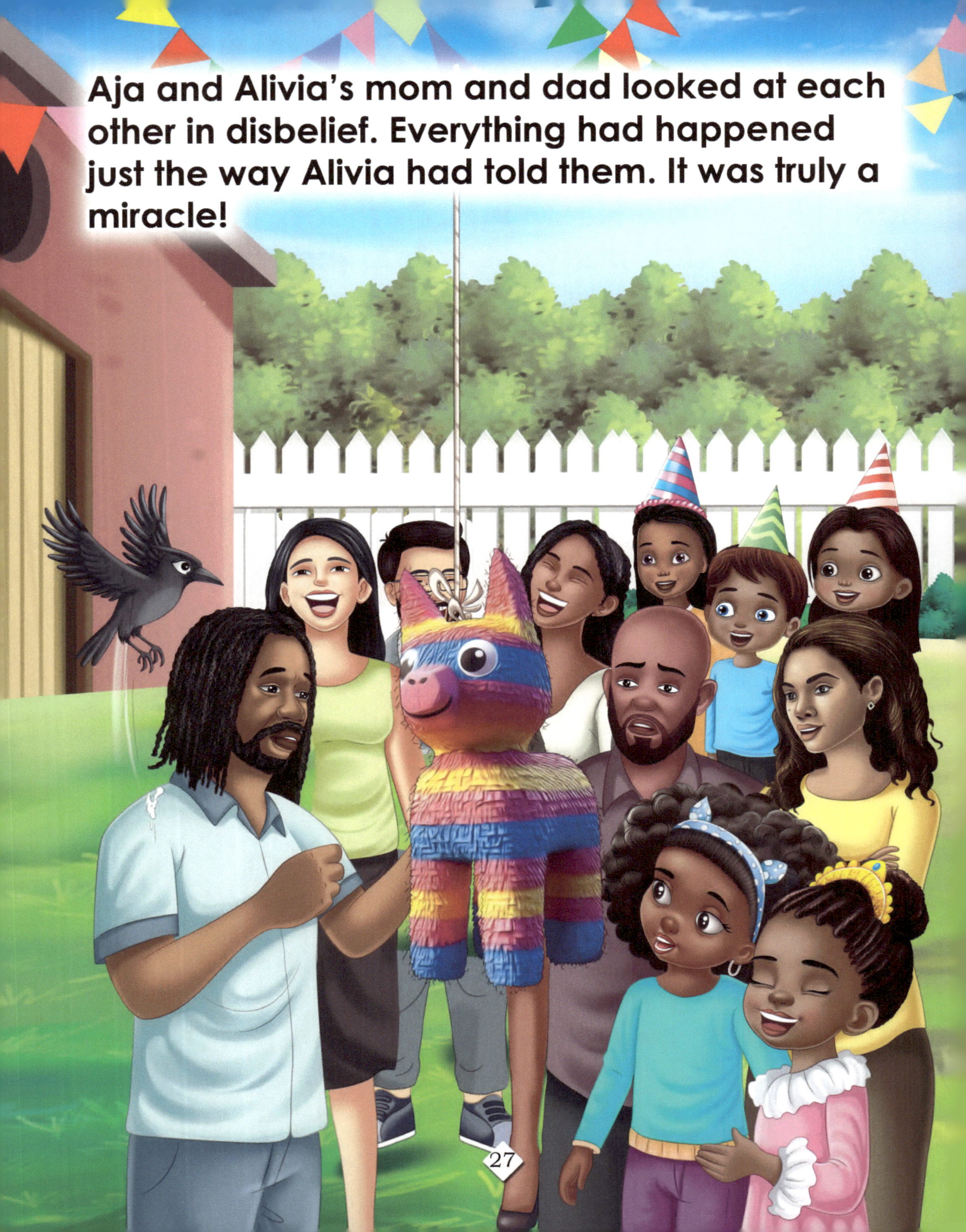

Aja and Alivia's mom and dad looked at each other in disbelief. Everything had happened just the way Alivia had told them. It was truly a miracle!

"Thank you so much, Daddy!" Alivia said, hugging her dad. "You made my birthday so special! I do have a question though. Didn't you feel like we have done all of this before? That's what people call deja vu, right?"
"Maybe it's because it's such a special day," said her dad, still being in denial.

That night, Alivia's dad had the strangest dream. In his dream, God told him that all of Alivia's memories had been visions of their future life. She had wanted to spend time with her dad so much that she had asked God to give her a sign. Alivia's dad could feel how much Alivia loved him. He also loved her so much. In fact, she was the most special person in his life. And Alivia's Dad loved her more than anything in the whole world.